TEN-DOLLAR BILLS

BY MADDIE SPALDING

The Child's World®
childsworld.com

Published by The Child's World®
1980 Lookout Drive • Mankato, MN 56003-1705
800-599-READ • www.childsworld.com

Photographs ©: Brian McEntire/Shutterstock Images, cover
(foreground), cover (background), 1 (foreground), 1 (background),
20 (bottom); Shutterstock Images, 5; Steve Stock/Alamy, 6, 7;
Vander Veiden/iStockphoto,9; iStockphoto, 10–11, 16–17, 20
(middle); John Kwan/Shutterstock Images, 13; Jill Battaglia/
Shutterstock Images, 15, 20 (top); Georgios Art/iStockphoto, 19;
Red Line Editorial, 22

Design Elements: Brian McEntire/Shutterstock Images; Ben Hodosi/
Shutterstock Images

ISBN 9781503820104
LCCN 2016960503

Printed in the United States of America
PA02336

ABOUT THE AUTHOR

Maddie Spalding writes and
edits children's books. She lives in
Minnesota.

TABLE OF CONTENTS

CHAPTER ONE

WHAT IS A TEN-DOLLAR BILL?

Ten-dollar bills are a type of money. Ten one-dollar bills make one ten-dollar bill. The Bureau of Engraving and Printing (BEP) makes ten-dollar bills. Bills are made from cotton and **linen**.

The BEP makes nearly two million ten-dollar bills each year.

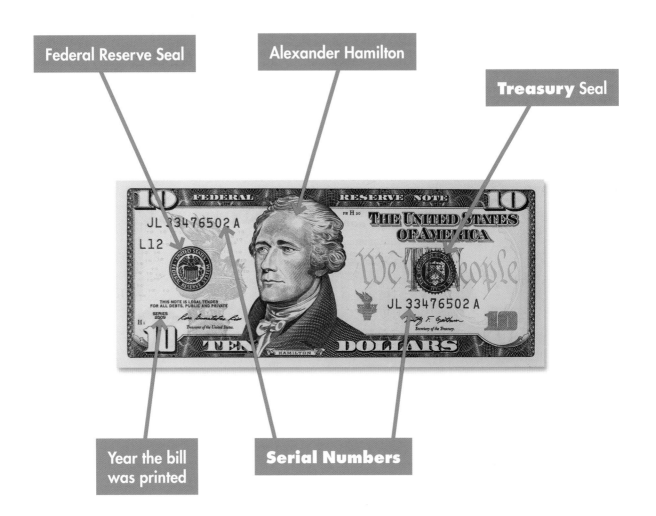

Federal Reserve Seal

Alexander Hamilton

Treasury Seal

Year the bill was printed

Serial Numbers

Alexander Hamilton is on the front of the ten-dollar bill.

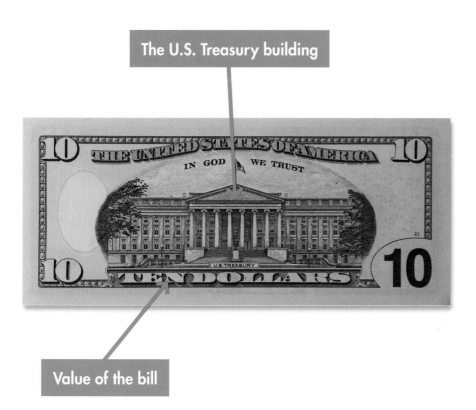

The U.S. Treasury building

Value of the bill

The U.S. Treasury building is on the back.

CHAPTER TWO

SECURITY FEATURES

Each ten-dollar bill has a security thread. This thread glows orange under **ultraviolet** light.

Why do you think there is a torch on the front of the ten-dollar bill?

The Statue of Liberty's torch is on the left side of the ten-dollar bill.

The watermark of Alexander Hamilton's face can be seen on the back left side of the ten-dollar bill.

The ten-dollar bill also has a hidden image. This is called a watermark.

Another image of Alexander Hamilton can be seen when the bill is held up to a light.

Ten-dollar bills also have serial numbers. These security features make it more difficult for people to make fake ten-dollar bills.

Why do you think some U.S. bills have different security features than others?

There are green numbers on a ten-dollar bill. These are called
serial numbers.

CHAPTER THREE

THE HISTORY OF THE TEN-DOLLAR BILL

The first U.S. ten-dollar bills were made in 1861. Abraham Lincoln was on the front. He was the 16th president of the United States.

A bison was put on the ten-dollar bill in 1901. A female figure named Columbia was on the back.

Former president William McKinley appeared on the ten-dollar bill in 1902. He was the 25th president of the United States.

Many people have been on the front of the ten-dollar bill. President Andrew Jackson was put on the front of the ten-dollar bill in 1914. Jackson was the seventh president of the United States.

Alexander Hamilton replaced Andrew Jackson on the bill in 1929. Hamilton has been on the front of the ten-dollar bill ever since.

How are the images on the front and back of the ten-dollar bill related?

ALEXANDER HAMILTON

was the first secretary of the U.S. Treasury (1789–1795). He helped the government handle its money.

1901 U.S. ten-dollar
bill

1861 The first U.S. ten-dollar bills were made. Abraham Lincoln was on the front.

1902 U.S. ten-dollar
bill

1902 William McKinley was put on the ten-dollar bill.

1914 Andrew Jackson was put on the front.

1929 Alexander Hamilton first appeared on the ten-dollar bill.

2003 U.S. ten-dollar
bill

1990 The U.S. Treasury began adding security features to the ten-dollar bill.

★ The ten-dollar bill shrank in size in 1929. The U.S. government needed to cut costs during the Great Depression. This was a time of financial decline in the United States from 1929 to 1939.

★ Thirteen people have appeared on the U.S. ten-dollar bill. Three of them were U.S. presidents.

★ The U.S. Treasury plans to reveal new designs for the back of the ten-dollar bill in 2020. The designs will honor leaders of the women's rights movement.

★ The average lifespan of a ten-dollar bill is 4.5 years.

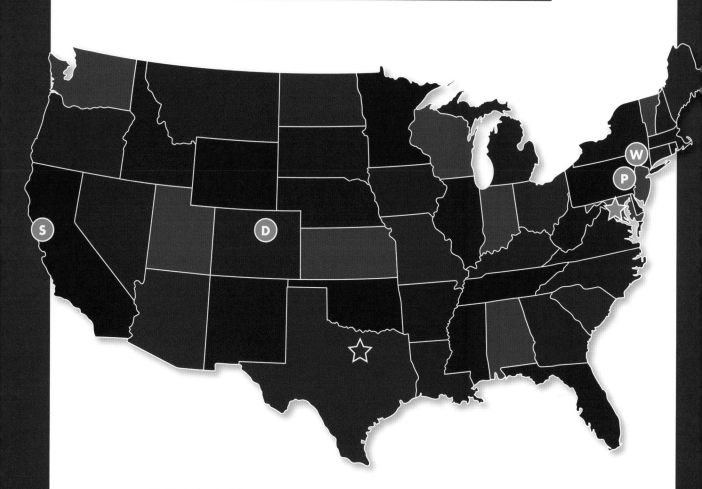

BUREAU OF ENGRAVING AND PRINTING OFFICES

⭐ Fort Worth, Texas

⭐ Washington, DC

COIN-PRODUCING MINTS

Ⓓ Denver, Colorado—Produces coins marked with a D.

Ⓟ Philadelphia, Pennsylvania—Produces coins marked with a P.

Ⓢ San Francisco, California—Produces coins marked with an S.

Ⓦ West Point, New York—Produces coins marked with a W.

linen (LIN-uhn) Linen is a strong type of cloth. Ten-dollar bills are made from cotton and linen.

serial numbers (SEER-ee-ull NUM-burz) Serial numbers are numbers that identify something. Ten-dollar bills have serial numbers.

Treasury (TREZH-ur-ee) A Treasury is a part of a government that is in charge of a country's money. The U.S. Department of the Treasury is in charge of money in the United States.

ultraviolet (uhl-truh-VYE-uh-lit) Ultraviolet is a type of light. Security threads on ten-dollar bills glow orange under ultraviolet light.

IN THE LIBRARY

Dowdy, Penny. *Money*. New York, NY: Crabtree, 2009.

Jozefowicz, Chris. *10 Fascinating Facts about Dollar Bills*. New York, NY: Children's Press, 2017.

Kulling, Monica. *Alexander Hamilton: From Orphan to Founding Father*. New York, NY: Random House, 2017.

Schuh, Mari C. *Counting Money*. Minneapolis, MN: Bellwether, 2016.

ON THE WEB

Visit our Web site for links about
ten-dollar bills: childsworld.com/links

Note to Parents, Teachers, and Librarians: We routinely verify our Web links to make sure they are safe and active sites. So encourage your readers to check them out!

INDEX